Stories from Eden

Carla Martin-Wood

THE PINK PETTICOAT PRESS
Not your grandmother's poetry

Editorial Reviews

Stories From Eden by *Carla Martin-Wood* is a fascinating collection of poems probing life and the human condition. Here, the author surveys the complexity of *"what is left of . . . Eden"* (*Don't Tell the Children*). *On the Hill* provides a brilliant analogy and political statement about the chasm between those who are privileged and those who are not. And *The Stone Girl* captures the ultimate moment of a breathless tragedy in a way that invokes the dark mood and eeriness of Ray Bradbury's *Something Wicked This Way Comes*. This collection invites the reader to perceive aspects of character and experience that reveal truths pertinent to an evolving planet and our spiritual selves.

— Wendy A. Howe, Freelance writer, Pushcart Prize nominee, former editor of *The Baroque Review*

In this 50th anniversary year of Rachel Carson's classic, *Silent Spring*, Carla Martin-Wood has devoted the entire first section of her newest collection to the environment. If Carson's book was a wakeup call, *Shadows over Eden*, eleven poems in Martin-Wood's *Stories from Eden*, is a blistering, yet mournful plea on behalf of Gaia and her children. *Are you scared yet?* unsparingly reminds us of the unspeakable poison we have allowed the oil industry to visit upon Earth: "across the bayou/ the hollow lament of mission bells/ prays without words." *Spring, anyhow* concludes the section in a fervent call to recognize that, no matter how careless we are with our Earth, it struggles mightily to persist with its gifts for us: "for it is spring anyhow/ in this place we are destroying/ it is spring anyhow/ that tries to dance arthritic/ through these limbs/ where nothing seems too heavy to bear/ nor no burden so oppressive/ as gardens lost/ as these blessings/ fragile and forgotten." Martin-Wood's voice is never more clear nor more insistent than when she speaks on this crucial subject.

— Margot Brown, Editor, Fortunate Childe Anthologies, Pushcart Prize nominee, author *Leave of Absence* (The Pink Petticoat Press)

It takes an incredibly brave poet to challenge any form of received wisdom and query the existing mythos. Carla Martin-Wood is such a poet. When she tells us in "Unknown Angels" that *I question the sacred nature/ of those wondrous ones/ mysterious and invisible/ useless,* we know she's not joking. This is a poetry collection crammed with questions — some capable of responses, most not. But they are being asked anyway, and in such original imagery that we are captivated, even though some of us might also admit to a frisson of unease. *I must wonder/ to whom does God turn/ for absolution* ("At the confessional"). What a disquieting idea! Carla Martin-Wood's poetry cannot be read without a seat-shifting sense of discomfort — because she is upending the reader's preconceptions; because she has dared to turn "Wait a minute, you've got it wrong" into an art form. Her command of language leaves us in no doubt that poetry is her soul's offering.

— Brenda Levy Tate, Pushcart Prize nominee, author of *Wingflash* (The Pink Petticoat Press)

In *Stories From Eden,* Carla Martin-Wood gleans for us profound truths from life's eternal mysteries, artfully exposing the devil in his details, and casting aspersions on invasive crows ravaging hallowed cherry trees. Another amazing collection, presented with the same moxie and panache for which she is widely known.

— Kevin Heaton, author of *Family's Family* (White Violet Press)

An ingenious compilation of poems encompassing a wide-range of themes that transition effortlessly from the personal to the universal in the blink of an eye. *Stories from Eden*, by Carla Martin-Wood is a stunning collection in which life is not only examined, but somehow shrewdly explained, with breathtaking verse that rejoices in the grace of the human spirit, in poems like *Don't Tell the Children* and *Unknown Angels.* In language that can only be admired, we are nearly broken with grief by the poem *The Stone Girl*: "coins still clenched /eyes wide with surprise," only to be elevated by the beauty of willful acclaim in *Bedtime Story* "The bird needs not a hymnal/ to sing its tune." Martin-Wood's voice is not only commanding in this latest collection, she guides the reader through a stimulating journey, breaking through facades like a sculptor forging a statue, meticulously carving away the superfluous until we can only marvel at what remains.

— Carol Lynn Stevenson Grellas, multiple Pushcart Prize nominee, author of *Epistemology of an Odd Girl*, (March Street Press)

In gratitude

My thanks to Wendy, "Mitzi" and Brenda

for their roles as midwives in the birthing of this book.

Dedication

This book is for the serpent,

without whom Genesis would have been

the last book.

The Poems

Shadows over Eden

Stories from Eden

The Poems

Dwellers in Eden

The Poems

Songs from Eden

To my readers

When I asked a trusted friend and exceptionally gifted writer to review this text, Brenda Levy Tate defined the essence of this work with honesty and keen insight. She summarized the intent and potential of these poems as follows:

This is a poetry collection crammed with questions – some capable of responses, most not. But they are being asked anyway, and in such original imagery that we are captivated, even though some of us might also admit to a frisson of unease. Carla Martin-Wood's poetry cannot be read without a seat-shifting sense of discomfort. Because she is upending the reader's preconceptions; because she has dared to turn "Wait a minute, you've got it wrong" into an art form. Her command of language leaves us in no doubt that poetry is her soul's offering.

For all its unnerving insight into the broken legends we have created and then clumsily reconstructed, the poet's gift is wrapped in beauty. When we open it, an abused child (or planet) might huddle inside – next to a Medusa or Lilith reminding us that Eve is strictly derivative. Once unfolded, none of the old stories can be put back. Instead, they must be reshaped until they're accurate and true, even if some of the glimmer fades.

Reshape them, we must, or bear the consequences. Cast by the great myths we have created for ourselves, the long shadows of Eden reach out across millennia to tease at the edges of our dreams of peace and progress or stir guilt for our abuse of this planet and our treatment of each other.

While the great myths teach us truths, when believed to be sacrosanct and taken literally, they cause chaos. If we consider the story of Adam and Eve in Genesis, we see the root of the problem.

They received divine orders to *be fruitful and increase in number; fill the earth and subdue it . . . to rule over the fish of the sea and the birds of the air and over every living creature that moves on the ground.* The children of Adam and Eve have certainly fulfilled that edict. We have not only been fruitful – we have overpopulated the planet. We have more than subdued the earth – we have brought it to its knees, while denizens of the deep and the air fall prey to our progress.

If we are to survive, we must restore what we've stripped away – and in the process, just maybe we can learn to get along with each other. Whether we evolve a sense of responsibility to the planet and all its inhabitants through a religious belief system or an internal code of ethics, we know we must make changes, or risk losing our children's inheritance and what is left of this Eden.

And then, there's that old serpent. Brenda continues:

. . . Even if we are forced to acknowledge that the snake was right all along and that Eve's only sin was her craving for knowledge, which has dogged her children's footsteps ever since. The book's dedicatory note to the serpent makes one thing clear: without temptation, betrayal and desire for the unattainable, there can be no progress.

It took that first bite of the alluring apple, that first betrayal of authority, to taste the knowledge that would set the wheels of science, art and the history of mankind – with all our failures, flaws, and glory – in motion. It was, quite literally, a necessary evil.

Hence, I would add that the serpent has another role in my dedication – as a sustaining force in the garden of humanity, as a procurer of future chapters to be written and acted upon.

As Joseph Campbell emphasizes in his great work, *The Power of Myth*, ancient cultures revered the serpent as a symbol of wisdom, healing, regeneration, and spiritual revelation. Whether we find it wrapped about Eden's apple tree or coiled around the Caduceus, we must respect its necessity. If we cannot embrace forbidden secrets and attain knowledge of their origin and power, we cannot survive with dignity, shed our scales of ignorance, and regenerate ourselves and our planet.

Finally, this book is not meant to be didactic – if so, I'm preaching to myself as much as to anyone, for it is my own failure that informs the poems and inspires my personal journey. You'll find poems about the environment, socio-political issues and the failure by religion to give us answers, but you'll also find poems about the great myths that turn them topsy-turvy. I hope you find more than one reason to smile. And you'll meet some of the residents of Eden, whom I've been privileged to know.

I send this out into the world naked of excuses, but as a love letter to you all – and with the hope that it will leave you with questions, for I lay no claim to answers.

Carla Martin-Wood

Brenda Levy Tate is the author of *Wingflash* (The Pink Petticoat Press, 2011), *Cleansing* (Rising Tide Press, 2005) and *Beeline* (Lopside Press, 2007), and included in *Jailbreaks: 99 Canadian Sonnets* (Biblioasis 2008), an anthology of the editors' favorite Canadian sonnets of the past century.

Shadows over Eden

Are you scared yet?

Drifting over Eden
in this dark, ill-chosen hour
do you glance below
and see the shadows?

now that the oily wake of the rigs
suffocates bird and beast
now that it wanders its noxious path
through fertile wetlands
destroys future generations
smears flower, feather, reed

now that Wall Street's anointed
offer up unctuous cash
as though it will purchase back
all things winged and wondrous
and those that swam free
between the great coral ribs
of the mother

claw and fang are impotent
against this malignancy
and boats of hungry fishermen
a poor defense
against this vile armada

across the bayou
the hollow lament of mission bells
prays without words.

Too Late

It's too late
the alarm sounded long ago
but we didn't listen
let marketplace manlogic rule
preferred profits to prophecy
of tree huggers
and biologists
it's too late for talks
between the big oil bullies
and failed government
our wetlands have been sold out
shining green and gold
nursery to sea life
breath of an economy
suffocated
it's too late for the promenade
of kings and queens
of Mardi Gras
for the bead tossing throng
for the scent of magnolia
tinged with the stink of oil
petals soiled and black
it's too damned late
to be shocked
to be stunned
to make a stab at a comeback

in the quiet, cold darkness
of our hearts
we knew this all along
knew it was coming
with every drop of blood
in our tanks.

Don't tell Mama

Don't tell Mama
what we've done here
if she finds out
oh man
she's gonna be pissed

we were just playing
having a good time
and now just look at what we've done

oh man
look at the mess we've made
of her garden

oh man
look at how her pets died
starting with the birds
and now even the bees are leaving

oh man
look at how we made everything so dirty
with our toys
how the streams
look like a backed-up toilet
how the air
burns our eyes
how we've even broken
her thermostat

oh man
there may not be time to clean this up
no time to fix things
before she sees

oh man
she's gonna be mad

hey
do you think she knows already?
was that an earthquake
or was that her
shaking with rage?
was that a tornado
or was that her
getting ready
to clean house?
was that a tsunami?
or was that her
warming up
to give us the whipping of our lives?

oh man
Mama's coming
and she's pissed.

Don't tell the children

Don't tell them
how we ate snow ice cream
free of factory made contamination
piggybacked poison
with the snowfall

Don't tell them
how we drank from virgin streams
unsullied by our greed
how we swam crystalline waters
clear as our consciences

Don't tell them
how we picked blackberries
in the wild
let juice drip down our chins
without a toxic thought
how we climbed orchard trees
to steal unwashed cherries

Don't tell them
how we hiked untouched glory
watched a thousand suns set
in rainbowed splendor
unenhanced by airborne chemicals
that alter nature's palette
and photoshop our view

Don't let them know
about brightfeathered wonders
and Amazonian treasures
lost to marketplace manlogic

Don't tell them
how bees left
the flowers on their own
and how the flowers went down, too
with nothing but a lucky wind
to spread their kind

Don't let them know
there were rivers
without warnings
and oceans
thick with life
and don't let them know
about coral castles undersea
It would be too cruel.

As we turn photographs to the wall
when a loved one passes
let us burn the images
of all once-living things
as each species disappears
let it be done
lest the children know
what was lost.

Like all good politicians
let us cover our tracks
hide the evidence
of our incalculable avarice
our limitless waste
our misnamed progress
our indifference
lest the children know
our greed.

Let us remove all stories
of creation from all sacred texts
lest the children know our guilt.

Don't tell them
how we betrayed our duties
how we squandered their inheritance
how so little now is left
of their Eden.

Way of the Raven

Skylarks never contemplated
benefits of asphalt
flown to shrinking woodlands
they compose hymns
of loss and longing
to Gaia

Ravens are another matter
appreciating occasional
squirrel meets Goodrich
or hare outfoxed
by Volkswagen

Nevermore crows
scavenge amongst tall grasses
remove that which fouls
sweet country air
but congregate
along this highway
raspy caws announcing
smoggy dawn
they leisurely await
the next convenient kill

Nor can we blame these
bold opportunists
who make the best
of progress
our fast food delivery
of carrion
we too lazy to walk
whose faith lies

in the Mórrígan
sprawling cities
that feed her warlords
highways between
that carry us
swift-commuting
angels of death
delivering our message of
doom to chipmunk
hapless armadillo
and homeless lark

On weekends
making our escape
to the country
see them swagger
off the median
like they own the place
Hitchcock their heads
peer into windows
of cars stopped at red lights
take our measure
dream of bigger game.

On the hill

The Kwansan cherry tree
lifts branches
thick with a thousand shades
of pink ruffles
yet even bees
stay away
butterflies
keep their distance
for thieving crows
have invaded
staked their claim
they people these limbs
in domination
the few
assert themselves
above the many

the tree
that has stood
for centuries
knows her limbs vacant
of nesting bluebirds
silent
happy buzz and flutter
gone
for her
there is no springtime
resurrection

obsidian feathers foul
roseate brilliance
tyrants strut

up and down their perches
caw
harsh edicts
mindless
shit the earth below
careless
without regard for the masses
that crawl there

but ants burrow
worms tunnel
squirrels chatter
and at night
turtles like army helmets
move in slow reconnaissance
burrowing owls
peer from foxholes
hoot a message
relayed to barred owls
canker takes root
they bide their time.

Kwansan cherry trees cover Washington, DC, a gift from the Japanese people. The Kwansan is considered the Tree of the Sacred Mountain.

The Least of These
Matthew 25: 34-40

The least of these
have faces
we don't see
they are coins in the poor box
shadows in the doorway
meager fire beneath a bridge
our worst fear becomes
the face we give them

The least of these
had a mother daughter grandchild
college degree
liked bubble baths
sang karaoke
fought for his country
sold cars
liked chocolate
grew roses
ran a business
taught Sunday School

The least of these
got sick
lost a job
was laid off
lost a baby
drank too much
shot up
was abandoned
got old
had Alzheimers Parkinsons Schizophrenia
took too much time

too much money
too much trouble

The least of these
are white black latino gay straight male female
someone's prodigal
pilgrim soul
a prediction
they have names
Ashley Bob Altheria Samuel Mike
but no one knows them

The least of these
will work for food
or fuck for a fix
are terrified angry hurt
don't recognize their reflections anymore
remember Christmas
remember family
can't remember happy
cry like a baby
when no one sees
can die of a disease
conquered decades ago
have learned to fear hope
more than status quo

The least of these
hunger for respect
a job
a bath
clean water
clothes
a corner to hide in
sleep

a day of not looking behind them
acknowledgement
of their humanity

The least of these
belong to us
in shame or glory
inasmuch as we open our hearts
inasmuch as we close them.

May 21, 2011

Climbing Jacob's Ladder
no way
nor Ezekiel's wheel
they're all heading upward
on a shiny red elevator
bound for Heaven

they can hardly wait
for the world to end

they're so excited
they've forgotten
to tie their shoelaces
see how they stumble
and push into each other
rushing to be first
among the salvaged

they've forgotten the garden
how to tend the flowers
and the old man
selling pencils on the corner
just another casualty
no time to clean the fridge
and give its contents
to starving souls
in the alley behind the old church

and all that money poured
into stained glass windows
and gyms where teens
can work off sexual energy
all of that goes up in smoke

when Jesus comes
to meet them in the air

down below
all us heathens wait
thinking about how much loot
will be left behind
how many resources may be saved
now that there aren't so many
church bulletins to print
so many potlucks to cook
and how so many empty houses
will await the homeless

yessiree, sir
right this way
got your ticket to heaven
just climb onboard
we'll take care
of what's left behind.

May 21, 2011 The 2011 end times prediction made by American Christian Radio host Harold Camping stated that the Rapture and Judgment Day would take place on May 21, 2011, and that the end of the world would take place five months later on October 21, 2011.

Unknown angels

I am one aware of angels

not the litany of mellifluous names
that slip like holy water
drooled from the lips
of the boring blessed

nor those adorning
ceilings of great cathedrals
lost in perpetual flight
eyes vacant
from gazing on glory

nor those posted with flaming swords
vigilant against knowledgeable humans
barring them from Eden
with its sinuous inhabitants
and dangerous trees

I question the sacred nature
of those wondrous ones
mysterious and invisible
useless
with their ivory fingers
and pristine robes

those angels I see
frescoed on my inner eyelids
just before I sink to slumber
rise up with dirty fingernails
ready to do the job
fierce in strength
and less spectacular

like the African angel
not allowed to attend
my grandmother's church
who risked her life
to save a white child
from a pervert

and the elderly angel
who had a stroke
wrestling his daughter's abuser
to the floor

or Hell's Angels
in black leather
who slammed a wife beater
against the brick wall of a church
in an alley one night
who swore his death
if he didn't leave town

I sing in praise
of hands-on angels
without hierarchy
or rote prayers
those whose sweat
doesn't smell of lilies
who die in their sins
and fall to dust
unknown.

At the confessional

Watching the line
of trembling penitents waiting
to rid their burdened souls of sin
like lusting after the pool boy
or not forgiving the Pope
for his complicity
in child molestation

I must wonder

to whom does God turn
for absolution
when He smites a nation
or sends angels to slay firstborns
or turns a woman to salt
for looking back
or when He gambles with Satan
over some wretched Job

when He turns His godly countenance aside
and does nothing
while the ungodly plays out
like genocide or toddlers burning in a daycare
or a homeless man freezing to death
bundled in discarded Christmas wrap
as an alley fills with snow

is there some Uber God
who listens to His mea culpas
for His almighty negligence
or when He curses
someone with cancer
or necrotizing fasciitis

His hippie Son must have been
such an enigma to Him
this Christ who healed
wounds inflicted by his Father
brought sight
to eyes his Father veiled
who stopped stonings
his Dad had ordered
that rebel soul
who preached peace
instead of plagues
and was crucified for his trouble
while crying out
Why have You forsaken me?

to whom does God confess
where does He go with His sin
while our laundry lists grow
and we search our hearts
for more to add

like the time I grabbed a burger
on Good Friday
or when my neighbor
skipped an obligatory mass
to ladle watery soup into bowls
for the hungry.

Spring, anyhow

These limbs are laden with blossoms
but do not break
they obliterate the sky
with pink tenacity
though acid rain falls
and petals cling pallid and frail
to the black bark

nothing breaks
this roseate morning
though the petals are leaden
and their weight
has become everything
for losing even one
is immediately noticeable
and leaves a hollow place
of echoed prayers
and remembered flutings of birds

nothing breaks here
but bends and sways
in hurricane winds
man-blighted roots hold firm
though the sad earth
quakes and trembles
and at night the moon
caught in this net of branches
holds the sea still
her eyes remembering
what swam beneath
what flew above

for it is spring anyhow
in this place we are destroying
it is spring anyhow
that tries to dance arthritic
through these limbs
where nothing seems too heavy to bear
nor no burden so oppressive
as gardens lost
as these blessings
fragile and forgotten.

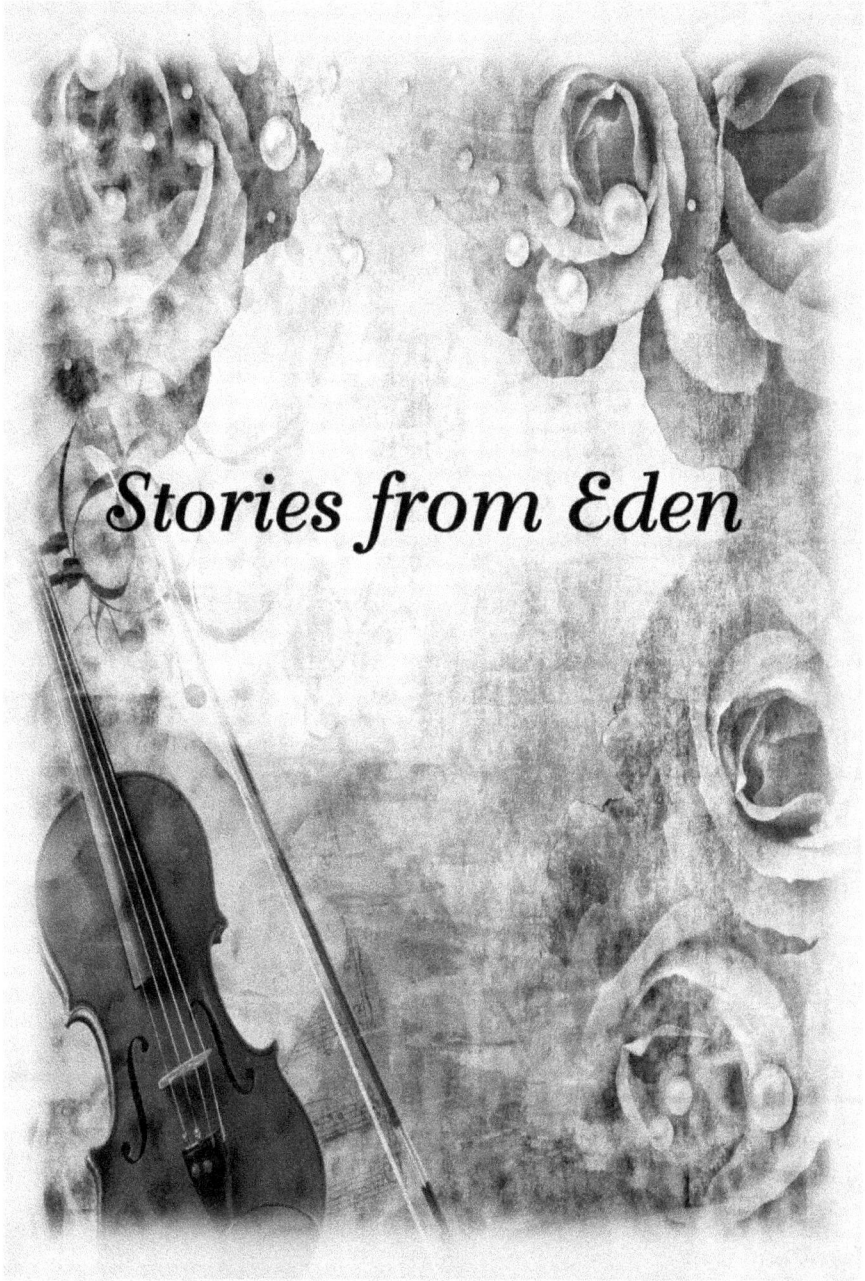

Stories from Eden

Medusa

It's not as though I were the first
to trade my shining curls for coils
or follicles for fangs
to share a taste
for all things wise and serpentine
after all, it was your Eve
who dared the Knowledge Tree
with its ripe fruit
she, too, was faced
with all the hair-brained
myths men make
when they can't reconcile
a woman's beauty
with a well-endowed IQ
the same as those
who claim that I was cursed
when truthfully, this stunning coif
is shrewd Athena's gift
these slithering dreads that petrify
yet turn men soft
where it counts most to them
my friends here threaten none
though I'll admit
a cowlick now and then
when it's deserved
and as for Freud
there's little phallic
to be found in women's wisdom

Beware, beware
my lovely face
my writhing hair
but know each night

these serpent fangs
sink deep into my brain
there to impart
sweet venom
bitter knowledge
of men with flaccid will
and stony heart.

The Stone Girl

In a local churchyard, there stands an old statue. A little girl runs, a look of mild surprise on her face, six pennies embedded in her palm. She died in 1950, and this poem is based on the story people still share hereabouts.

Carnival on wheels
the ice cream lady approaches
hair coiled
serpentine
calliope music
blasting its siren call
to every child

Marisol jumps rope
life cartwheels inside her
she is perpetual joy
singing her five years
of olly-olly-oxenfree
Marco
Polo
red rover red rover
send Marisol over
ring around the roses
I'm a little Dutch girl
dressed in blue
all fall

down the drive she runs
Nonna! Ice cream!

Nonna presses six pennies
into her eager palm
and Marisol scatters
like blossoms
like butterflies

running toward
ice cream
and the lady
with sinuous hair
who beckons
between the old blue Studebaker
and Mr. Cannon's Oldsmobile

and then
(incomprehensible)
it is Breugel's Icarus
the world just going on
like it's nothing extraordinary
as a wingless child
takes flight
while Mrs. Rosario tends her garden
and Mr. O'Malley complains

Marisol rises
in slow motion
like a silent movie
but in heartstopping reality
a scream of tires
the sudden fall
of a child with coins to spend

empty sandals
on the pavement
as though they wait
for her to put them on again

Marisol barefoot and silent
sprawled on the newly watered grass
of Mr. O'Malley's front yard

coins still clenched
eyes wide with surprise.

she lies in the family plot
where Uncle Tito
who sculpted gravestones
created an everlasting tribute

The Stone Girl
we've come to call her
six pennies embedded
in her marble palm
eyes crinkled in laughter
always running
toward the lady
with serpentine curls
who beckons
and the calliope music
of an ice cream truck
blasting its siren call.

Circe

Transforming men to swine was not a stretch;
I barely had to put the kettle on.
For inside every man, there lives a letch,
and each of them is far less brain than brawn.

There was no spell, no chant, no cauldron stirred;
I just suggested strolling on the shore.
One glance at my four nymphs, no magic word,
the switch was made, and they were men no more.

To tell the truth, I do regret this deed
although I found it humorous at first;
their appetites incessant I must feed,
and now it's I who find myself accursed.

Lilith

Who I am sneaks up on a man
though I can tell when he knows
by his nervous laugh
or the way he can't quite focus
on things like the stock market
or football scores
that infinitely pleasurable moment
when I know he's lost control

I never know
just what may tip him off
the candles
at the bottom of the stairs
always burning
though no one lights them
or the shadow of a lion
that prowls across the wall
perhaps, it's that ill wind
howling clear and cold
around the eaves
though it's hot August
and not a leaf is stirring
more often, it's those pale fingers
that trace words on the wainscoting
after dinner: *mene mene tekel* . . .

Along about then he realizes
I didn't come from any man's rib
and I'm no Eve
who needs a snake to tell her
what to do
hell, I planted the tree he crawled out of

I sing up tsunamis, baby
take your children
steal your soul
fuck with your dreams.

Eve

No petals to scent passively the breeze
or leaves to turn submissive toward the sun
no roots to hold me firmly in my place
no graceful frond — no seeds
I can tell you that garden expelled me for a misfit
long before its Gardener cast me out

And then, there was
The Voice

Shall I tell you what it was to listen?
How beyond impossible it was to turn away?

It was not the unexpected conversation
nor the surprise of intelligence within his eyes
that beguiled me
It was that he spoke to me at all
as though I were more
than an afterthought provoked to pacify
The Man
or a secondhand rib to cloak in lesser flesh

And it was that he seemed to know
the mysterious longing that rose unbidden
each time I saw the vixen nuzzling with her kits
or the ewe with her lamb

And that he knew with what boredom
I watched alone
flowers and fruit grown unaided
as the days droned on
same after same
no change, no end in sight

And so I took the fruit he offered
and found it sweet
a grace upon my tongue
and marveled at so many seeds

And desire quickened and crawled
deep in my belly for the first time

And I recalled the pink flesh of the fig
and sought her out, and took her leaves
to cover the surprise of rosy nipples
and the secret that awakened
warm and dark between my thighs
but it was never to hide from the Gardener
and his disfavour that I so adorned myself
I did it to entice The Man
that he might savour
that sweetness of my flesh
that he had never guessed

I didn't even mind
when the henchmen came with their fiery swords
to bind the garden gates
and cast us out

Truth to tell
I never liked strolling with the Gardener
always a pace behind him and The Man
never knowing
what they said
never knowing
what to say
never daring
to ask
never understanding
why I was something he thought of last

All said, all done
I'd do it again

just to feel that intoxicating rush of my blood
when I first knew
I could cause The Man to tremble
as I held him riding the night within me
or to see the sweet pursed lips of Cain
innocent and new
as he suckled at my breast
like the vixen with her kits so long ago

or to watch the thriving pomegranate tree
that sprouted up from those seeds
I carried with me

I never wept
and never lost a thing
they all have lied who said I fell
I didn't fall
from anywhere –

I leapt!

Genesis

It would make a magnificent story
for men to tell
soothing each other
placing blame
hell
they'd make a religion of it

how she was made
all soft and pliant
shaped around his useless rib
as though any part
of him
so weak and undesirable
could contribute to the force of nature
she had become
will strong, mind bright

his constant fawning made her ill
she'd never stoop
to curry the favor
of a God who created and degraded her
simultaneously

seeds of that fruit
were all she cared to take
she snatched up a bit of lemon balm
rubbed it along her arms
to ward off insects
that would surely come now

lips pursed
brow furrowed
she looked back for a salty moment

at the unwashed glory of it all
the full-out great deception
it would soon become

later there would be angels
flanking the gates
hellfire and damnation
brought about by a single woman
betrayed by intelligence
stories to soothe
the little boys

the body of evidence against her
would later show
how she pulled away
from the garden
head thrown back
laughing in the wind
tires screeching
leaving easy tracks
to follow.

Summation to the Jury

He told her not to eat
from that compelling tree
glowing all incandescent
in the sun of Paradise
which fruit would bestow
extra-special godlike
knowledge of good and evil

thus, the all-knowing
set her up to fall

she was beguiled
like any child
by the offering
that hung so ripe and ready

but in this serpentine seduction
there is a flaw

before the eternally maligned
tasted the damning fruit
she was non compos mentis
without capacity to divine
good from evil

until that first fatal swallow
of god juice
she was innocent
as any kid
reaching for a cookie
that smelled of chocolate
warm from the oven

yet behold the unjust
condemnation meted out
that mythic day

when time lurched
and dark gods hovered
in collective silence
a conspiracy of serial killers
they retreated
to stoke hell's furnaces
with brimstone heat.

Magdalen

And who was I, that I should love a god?
A woman made of earth and warm desire,
who in his dusty footsteps humbly trod
a pace behind, yet stoked the gossips' fire

with my mere presence. I was ever mute
when questioned by disciples at his side,
and jealous of his favor, they'd dispute
my right to his affection. They denied

the place I never felt I truly owned.
Though still, when angels rolled away the stone
that early Easter morning, he chose me
to witness first his stunning victory.

Yet be it miracle, or be it art,
his *noli me tangere* crushed my heart.

Vampyre

for Aidan

Time was
we knew evil
when it came for us
fangs bared, breath reeking ,
of blood and wickedness
hideous faces
black-lipped and pale
ready to drag us to hell
we cowered behind
our bags of popcorn
barely breathing
until the villagers rose up
with torches and pitchforks
and Van Helsinged the villain
to eternal damnation

Afterward
we wandered home
feared their dust
might reanimate
clutched sharpened pencils
from our bookbags just in case
touched crosses round our necks
felt sorry for the Goldsteins and Brombergs
who had only Stars of David to count on
went to Mass next morning
drank the blood and ate the flesh
of Him who died and rose again
to give us all eternal life
and save us every one
till the next Friday night cinema
wakened the darkness
within us again

Older now
I find things aren't as clear
boundaries less defined
those paragons of malevolence
have been upgraded
like everything else
a glamorous evilution
amongst the enclave of the doomed
oh, they are damned
beautiful, these rock star
lost boys, bad boys
leather-clad and lovely studs
shining on their boots
compelling as black roses
sweetly decadent
they come
bearing dark gifts
eyes that drink us
in to promises of eternal forever
in the suburbs
where no one has acne
or morning breath
let alone the bad taste to die

Finally
we wander home
still enchanted
by their flowing hair
long, pale fingers and hard
muscled arms to embrace us
in some ecstasy
no mortal man could deliver
till every disillusioned Mina
rips off her Confirmation cross
and tosses the garlic salt

from her cupboard
to sit by the window
in clouds of diaphanous curtains
throat bared and vulnerable
dreaming of moonlit seduction
with no one
to save her.

Bedtime story

For my granddaughter

Oh, yes – child.
I could tell you another story
pen another poem
about the great-grandmother
who did not live
to know you

Reveal to you the miracle
that her pale skin
was not singed
by hair that flamed out
Pre-Raphaelite in glory
like the sun

I could untie the riddle
of her hands
how they glided
across piano keys
ivory on ivory
swans on a fairytale lake

I could tell you
how her closets brimmed
with sequined confections
a hundred hats
a thousand shoes
worthy of Cinderella

Oh, I could once-upon-a-time her
with salty stories
of lovers mysterious
spindles and golden straw

poisoned apples
and princes who never showed up

I could tell you
how she walked
graceful as Anderson's Mermaid

But to tell the truth
it's all water now
slipped shining
through the fingers
of a daughter
who clings in vain
to a myth she made
of ink and paper
to keep her safe
while growing up
with no hands to rock her cradle
or cool a fevered brow
no time to tell a story
like I am doing now
no maternal eyes
to smile in pride
at school plays
or birthday parties

Listen, child:
years apart from her now
magnify the memory
out of all proportion
in my brain
but climb up and listen
I'll tell it all by heart

the bird needs not a hymnal
to sing its tune.

Comet

for Kathy Allison

A child who loved myths,
summer evenings I would search
amongst the stars to find
Andromeda between the clouds,
sweet arms lifted, though in chains,
or altruistic Chiron with his bow,
honored there forever,
celestial and eternal monuments,
reminding us from whence we came
and what, with grace, we might attain.

Yet, on that sleepy August afternoon,
when Kathy called me up the hill to play,
I still refused. Four to my nine years,
I thought myself too old for her,
and too grown-up for paper dolls.
So Kathy went her solitary way,
learned how swiftly fire can leap
from match to flesh,
how paper dolls can burn,
lingered without hope for days,
hers, the first coffin I would see,
she, who made death real to me,
and still I hear the sound
her mother made.

Tonight I hurried home to watch
as Comet Lulin streaks the sky, and yet
instead, through these late tears I saw
a four-year old run helpless

down a neverending hill,
an ever-living torch,
fire fanning out like wings against the night,
immortal in my darkness.

Kong

Each time Kong falls
from his pinnacle
that silent thunderous
slow motion descent
to earthshaking destruction
I weep
whether in shadows
of a darkened theatre
or in my living room
watching it on TV
I don't bother hiding
the tear that slides down
unashamed

there's something hopeless
about those bullying planes
lethal insects metallic and unfamiliar
circling his massive form
the great beast helpless
to fend off man's design

there's something tragic
in his enormous trusting eyes
those whirls of amber iris
where gossamer clad
Ann Darrow stands
Beauty reflected

a story so lucid
the simplest child understands
how a Beast could love

how Beauty chooses her own
is not for sale
a bawd to be used or coached
by some pimp director

how Beauty and Beast
are always intertwined
and fall as one

how when the great Kong plummets
we all fall down
our shame resonating
in the drone of planes
the staccato of guns.

Gwenhwyfar to Lancelot from the convent

I will not forget
that you were Solstice
on the hillside of my life
as I approached its crest
through grasses drenched
in morning light
where fate unrolled
its carpet before me
nor that for a space
brief as a candle flicker
we lingered in sweet idolatry
of each other
before I began my descent

through years that distance us
you should know
that after evening prayers
when sisters safely sleep
and when the spirit flies away in slumber
all fetters on the heart released
my feet still dance
a glad return
in dreams or reverie
to that place we made
that magickal dominion
long lost to penance
and dire reality

that Camelot.

Immortal

Once arrogant arbiters
they roamed Olympus
and with precision aim
struck down hapless offenders
mortals who revealed too much
of truth or beauty

no more prideful
in youth or power
now they hide
behind foul weather
bitter winds relay their curses
from a darkened sky

winter must come
even for the gods
they cower in a shame of age
knowing not the human
relief of death
they finally understand
their own fate
fear immortal decay

Olympian snows afflict
arthritic arms that no longer hurl
lightning bolts with any accuracy
toothless they shiver
squint through cataract fog
attack without regard to target
frustrated and furious
unleash broadscale mayhem
a random rage
of hurricanes, earthquakes, landslides
and the occasional tsunami

here below
we soldier on
promise to remember
tell our children the old stories
visit temple ruins
miss them
when we have no one
to blame or praise
and feel a little sorry.

Wicked

for Jackie

Metro Goldwyn Mayer got it wrong.
Unlike that scarecrow with the prissy gait,
I'm here to sing a different little song;
I'm here to set the bloody record straight.

Those ruby slippers glittered and they glowed.
What's more, they were indubitably mine.
Not Jimmy Choo nor Manolo could boast
stilettos more breathtakingly divine

And so my jealous sister made her move.
She dropped the house directly on my head,
then took my shoes and swore that she could prove
that, ding-dong-ding, the "Wicked Witch" was dead.

Ars Gratia Artis? My sweet ass!
The studio, complicit in her act,
allowed her to escape the whole morass,
residuals and earnings all intact.

A little wink, a slap upon the hand,
and she was free – the bitch got clean away,
while I nursed a concussion and a brand
that still insists I'm wicked till this day.

Yet I got my revenge, it's true enough!
Those shoes rose to a dizzy-making height,
and when she put them on to strut her stuff,
the flying monkeys gave her such a fright,

she shattered both her ankles as she fell,
I snatched my slippers; now who sings the blues?
She finds herself in orthopedic hell,
while I dance in my steeltoe ruby shoes.

Dwellers of Eden

Love song for my brother

Edwin Ross Martin
May 30, 1954-January 7, 2010

Strangers in the nest, we were
unlike the other two
we shared Mother's milk
white skin, fine bones
it bound us for a time
born after me
I watched over you
till things changed
malignant childhood
Mother's toxic men and
Halloween when you were twelve
LSD on your candy
bad trick
bad trip
to the hospital
flashbacks
and bit by bit
superimposed
upon my face you saw
the Mother you abhorred
on yours, I saw
the Mother I adored
and the violence began
until my fear of you
bound up the love

Birmingham 1998
late summer concert
picnic blanket
chardonnay and Vivaldi
with a friend

till you appeared
shining in white linen
dark glasses
hair black as a crow's wing
your long-legged stride
stunned the provincials
into silence
damaged and damned
sinuous you descended
elegant among olive branches

We talked
and your red-brown eyes
flashed like Mother's
for a moment
I glimpsed
my tortured brother
chained within

You called
two weeks before you died
begged me to pick up
but I made myself stone
deaf, remembered loving you
was losing myself
in deep water
you were sucked under
hands reaching for help
but at my touch
you dragged me down
and I struggled
kicked hard
to escape

Three years gone now
I regret

at what expense
I saved myself
remember
how you walked away
beneath my window
rejected
shattering my heart
like no one else
in that rumpled tweed
shoulders hunched
head down
rain on your hair
like diamonds.

Joe Bar

Joe Bar is gone
four walls with no ceiling
to deter dreams
the four of us brought there
when we were eager
students of the world
who dissected every lecture
over Joe's dark ale
or read our poems
at the piano bar
looking out at kaleidoscope trees
third Thursday afternoon each November
the Beaujolais not nearly
as nouveau as we
damned children
of a Left Bank delusion
stuck in a steel town
sad and grey, no exit

Brad is gone
who made a pilgrimage to Rome
drank a toast to Keats for me
brought flowers for his grave
wrapped in a poem I wrote
because he knew I'd never make the trip
close-as-any-brother Brad
lean and strong and beautiful TA
strutting cocky before the class
cigarette a permanent accessory
tucked beneath the upper lip
don't ask, don't tell, closeted
in those days, but with me

hanging on his arm and every word
no one guessed his secret
till AIDS claimed him
when it barely had a name

Linda is gone
blonde and laughing
best friend pretender
who shacked up with the husband
of a woman who was dying
and slept her way
through halls of academia
dead by her own bloody hand
in a motel room
somewhere upstate

Marcus is gone
who aced Chaucer
and axed debate opponents
but flunked elementary ethics
bright-eyed politico
ark of our hopes
gone to rot in some prison
for malfeasance
if gold ruste, what shall iren do?

Joe Bar is gone
and where shall they go now
the ghosts of who we were
our beloved dart board gone long ago
the million holes around a pristine bull's-eye
pock-marked wainscoting that saw the best in us
replaced by glitter-embedded stucco
some redneck's design
intended to mimic heaven

Steinway kept to play a Pied Piper tune
for this newly opened inner city church
zealots who would have sent us all to hell
as though we couldn't find the way
ourselves.

Afghan lullaby

Legacy of the madman
betrayer of Ishmael
would-be slayer of Isaac
opiate of the masses
conceived in delusion
curse
your tune weaves its way
through DNA insanity
wrought in a minor key
thousands of years
descending
to be played out still

in Afghanistan
a mother casually breaks away
a small chunk of opium
feeds it to her child for breakfast
to lull him while she works
and his mind becomes
a murky pool
where elusive thought-fish
bloom like poppies
into suicide bombings
lovers stoned
burqa prisons
Taliban beheadings
pitiless darkness
as anesthetic alchemy
turns golden hope to lead.

Lady at the Window

For SG

I watched her at
the window of the asylum
a cardinal
female feathers drab and faded
seeing sky through glass
wind and earth
her birthright
she flung herself
against glass brutally
again and again
wings beating in
futile belief that
somewhere was a freedom
she could reach
world without ceiling
cornerless
once rider of winds
the hollow bones
in brittle effort
again and again
against glass

I could not hear the sound she made
(but I heard the rushing of my pulse
I could hang a sonnet on that rhythm)
and when she crashed
all splintered glass and bloody feathers
I knew what song was there.

For Mary Jane

This poem is for Mary Jane
who sits in the faded glow
of a sunset park bench
in early winter
whose true self
hides behind
closed and blue-veined lids
too thin to keep
the glare at bay

whose true self
is 9 years old today
and does not clutch
the handle of a walker
and never considered
Parkinson's tremble
but twirls
thirty-two measures
of petites rondes des jambes
across the park
in Joffrey-kindled dreams

whose true self
still loves Coney Island
Nathan's hot dogs
Choward's Violet Mints
pistachio ice cream
still waits the kiss
of a boy
who dates her sister
and sings doo-wop
on the corner
with his friends

this poem is for Mary Jane
who thought the shoes
were named for her
on black patent Sundays
in dresses of pale blue
she knelt at Mass
and took the Host
believing it was true

this poem is for Mary Jane
perpetually surprised
at her face
in the morning mirror
who walks to the park
to feed the birds
to close her eyes
to dance.

The suicide

I am not Lizzie lying here
sighing here drifting
in this float of flowers
petal coins soft upon eyes
that cannot unsee
I am no Ophelia

and not a mermaid
once knife-walking land lover
now fishtailed again
and broken
Hamlet-hearted sister
who could not do
what should be done
tangle-haired with jingle shells
awash in weedy brine
she waits for the quick dissolve
into a foam finale

nothing so romantic
no legend am I

only a woman mortal
soul heavy, bone weary
stone dropped into the chest for ballast
lured by the cold clean
sea-sky emptiness
dark hearts that once beat
to my rhythm
remembered now, leaden
weights they hold me
motionless save for waves
of Mother who rocks me to and fro
to a sadsong lullaby of scavengers

as I let it all go at last
into the salty void

before the riptide breaks me tears me
before another net ensnares me.

Old school

My grandmother lived in fear
that a black man would rape her
this was what black men did
she knew because everyone said so
and so many people couldn't be wrong

she was a good Christian woman
who nursed the sick
cared for the poor
a neighbor you could count on
kind and loving
always ready with a plate of her famous fried chicken
nourishing stew, or flowers from our garden
to visit, comfort, or mourn
and of all the people on our street
only she dared
to feed hoboes pale and begging
who jumped from the train
that ran behind our house
the only protrusion in their ragged pants
a knife
which she was sure they only carried for protection
poor things

but the black boy who came with his lawnmower
stood at the door and knocked
without answer
while she cowered in the living room
and the old black man with his mule-driven cart
heaped with fresh vegetables to sell
found no buyers at her house
though she said his tomatoes looked fine this year
and how she could tell even through the lace curtains

black women were another matter
Sally who was our nanny and lived in
Emma who did laundry on Mondays
young Anna Bee who did our ironing
and cleaned our house on Wednesdays
to earn money for school

but there was simply no excuse for black men
with their insatiable drive
to rape white women

everyone knew
that Johnny Mathis and Nat King Cole
couldn't sing gentle and soft like that
if they weren't part white
just listen to Little Richard
if you want to know
what black men are really after
or Jerry Lee Lewis
who had to have some black
in him somewhere
to wail all savage and wild

she would not listen to Dr. King
when he came along
with his peaceful words
nor did she know
how I followed him
marched to his drum
all over the south
when she thought I was safe
in school
nor did she know
about two black guys
who saved me

from a gang of rednecks
on Bourbon Street

when she was in her 80s
and living alone
she called me at my office
voice shaking
said how she took a cab from the grocer's
and with her failed vision
did not see
the cabbie was black
how she trembled in the backseat
till she arrived safely home
and locked her door
knowing he might remember her address
how she dreamed
he broke in last night
and stood over her
menacing

we laid my grandmother to rest
ninety-six years old
well loved
greatly missed
inviolate.

Prodigal

Her profile
pale and proud
almost recognizable
nothing else left
to give away
her former lofty position
save for the bag at her feet
battered ostrich leather
packed with relics
of fickle applause

the early train
whistles its low, sacred song
carries her across
an indolence of predawn bayou
frog chorus rising hypnotic
cane fields emerging from mist
and here and there
a lantern swings
flashes warm and welcome
through ragged darkness

coming home
to the city that bore her
so high
she flew
fallen now
broken
but undefeated

like her city
domicile of despair

saved by no god
saved by the orgy of life
that sustains it
survives
Betsy, Camille, Katrina
and this new, black grief of oil
stations of her cross
dark decades
of hell's rosary.

False spring

Dancing with clumsy grace,
the small, bare feet
of half-awakened spring
enter prematurely,
upstage winter for a day or two.

Skies grow sugary blue;
expectant sycamores, heavy with April,
shyly unveil green-gold buds,
and crocuses raise furtive, purple heads,
reconnaissance for less hardy troops to follow.

Giddy squirrels giggle,
and birds sing a cautious tune,
internal clocks aflutter,
they dream of cozy nests and fuzzy babies,
as memories of springs past
flood senses in calendared confusion.

Children clamor for freedom,
demand reprieve from February prisons,
trappings of coats and hampering galoshes,
whilst blushing Jennifer,
smitten with the boy-next-door,
presses to her lips the note he left her
places it on the music stand
sits at her piano
plays it perfectly by heart.

First

Down paths worn bare
by winter boots
we found a woodland
awash in blooms
burdened with April
and wild with spring
alive with hum of bees
and wings
gossamer and white
they fluttered by
all one
with blossomed trees
in heavy-honeyed prophecy
of fruit that could not be

there on the bridge
he enfolded me
as though I were a thing
of petals made and spring
that merest breath
might dissipate
and scatter to the winds
forever lost
and there we kissed
first, last
and not again

for fate let slip
the fragile string
that held us bound
to love stillborn
that breathed but once
and left our worlds
forlorn.

Song for Prometheus

who showed me a moon in a moonless sky,
and a dream in a dreamless sleep

Strangers will sift the ashes of our living
love, let us now make moments that will not burn

Come! Take me wandering through wide fields
out where the timothy grows so high
the breeze makes an ocean of it
making it peak and crest
making it flatten
and I shall wear my broad-brimmed hat
and be your lady for this hour
the briars will part to let us pass
then close like a gate behind

Come! Let me twine your arms and legs about
with honeysuckle, and you may weave clover
into my hair, and baby's breath

Come! I will take you
where blackberries grow thick clustered on the vine
where peaches blush ripe, heavy sweetness
eager to be stolen
Then shall we lie
stained all guilty with the juice
and learn the soft yielding
of pine beneath

I who have sung you songs of the moon
sing you a morning song
sweet as your mouth
upon my breast
warm as the honey

under your tongue
and you, my thief of sacred fire
steal this morning away from time
and I shall brave the sterile winter
bearing spring within me
like a child.

For Dean
Requiescat en pace

winter clouds stalked wooly
in spring's clothing, false
as green-plucked persimmons
that pucker and blister
lips too eager
yearning for premature sweetness
or scuppernongs
that burn the mouth
before juice runs
honey-ripe

some things get confused
bloom too fast
pollinate too early
die too soon

he pulled his old chevy
into the lot
behind the drugstore
hormones wild
hoping to cross a line

o, they were crazy
for each other

and it might have been
a memory
to tell a future son
or a cautionary tale
for a daughter

but winter made a quick return
revoking springtime's pass

and they left the heater running

morning light discovery
how they slept forever
curled together like babies
this sad-eyed Romeo
and his rosy-lipped Juliette

no bright pinioned angels
to sing them home
o, Mother
no magician's trick
to turn this milk to wine

his photograph on my dresser
these thirty years
like a fossil.

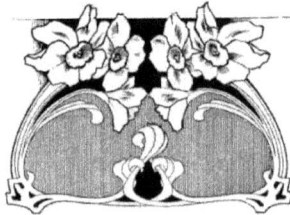

Beata Beatrix

(after the painting of Lizzie Siddal by Dante Gabriel Rossetti)

The famous heavy-lidded eyes now closed,
listless as the dead, she sits
in fading light, beside a stony wall,
alabaster shoulders suddenly demure
beneath a verdant drape.

She does not wait a midnight assignation
nor fawning artists to exalt
her beauty once again,
another pale Ophelia floating
in a river of flowers
~ no ~
she will not be the Blessed Damozel
who leans from heaven's bower,
for she has wandered here
to find a darker hour,
children forever now unborn,
dreams forever lost.

And what irony is this:
the dream-inducing drug
should snuff them out at last?

Let now the bloody dove descend;
now let the poppy fall.

Linguist
With love for my son

My own Demosthenes
when other babes said *Mama*
you grinned
dubbed me *Umbus*

using my heart
as a Rosetta Stone
I translated you to the world
the world to you

explained to others
that *frawkit*
was chocolate
and *tokkor*
doctor

the Voyager
with its golden disc
had nothing on you
frustrated
with the tangle of your tongue
you'd launch forth a mothership
of syllables so strange
they circle still
far reaches of the galaxy
and may some day
bring curious space aliens
to our world
in wonder

then came speech therapy
shouting at the sea

emerging from your cave
spitting out pebbles
you enunciated
flawlessly

time passed
and life
that snake
tail in mouth
has its jokes

macromolecular crystallography
Mom
not microbiology
how many times must I explain
neural receptors
blahblah
protein
blahblah
tau factor
blahblah
dephosphorylation
eee aye eee aye

ohhhhhh
for the days
of Umbus
and hot frawkit
before the speech tokkor
and the pebbles
and the cave.

Purple hull peas

Coming in from Papa's garden
baskets laden with purple hull peas
I was fascinated
by the way they climbed the trellis
as though someone had guided them
on their spiral path

now harvested
corkscrew tendrils still graced
purple and mottled pods
beloved still life
remembered

Grandmother and I
sat on the porch swing
big steel bowl between
we each had our method
hers wisely adapted
to arthritic fingers
mine, an exuberant eviction
as I popped out peas
with my thumbs

pong! pong!
metronomic rhythm
as peas met metal
hypnotic hollow song
that loosened tongues
and burdens

pong! pong!
no church bell
ever called me to confession
with more insistence

pong! pong!
as peas were freed
from constricting pods
a myriad
of tiny pink and purple eyes
staring out
from pale green

pong! pong!
I told her how I felt
out of place
skipping two grades
how everyone had boobs
except me

pong! pong!
Ricky Allison
got a butch haircut
and I think he's my boyfriend

why doesn't Mommy come home

pong! pong!
if my goldfish went to the sewer
when she died and got flushed
how come my dog went to heaven
and how sad I still felt
because I wouldn't play
paper dolls with Kathy
and then she died

pong! pong!

at last all the pods
lay open and empty

all their tasty burdens
yielded up

the face of my Mother Confessor
inscrutable as the Sphinx
no word of advice
just a nod now and then
a quiet yes or I know
leaving me lighter somehow
and strangely free.

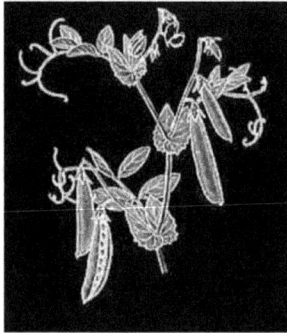

Fall

Summers past in the garden tree
I watched you swing from branch to branch
dangle one-footed
tumble
drop
then catch yourself mid-air
on a limb that
(almost)
wasn't there
and once a flash
the colour of your hair
plummeted toward earth
I heard a cry and caught my breath
but found you laughing in the shade
without a bruise –
There's Grace!

Now beneath that tree
with tears
you find unwanted tribute:
Feathers matted in the dirt
death no more anonymous.

And so you weep
that fang and claw
must stop the flight
and still the song
that gold-eyed fur
purred cozy into your heart all winter
must hissing spring toward violence.

There are not words
to make you believe

that purpose has its beauty, too
no reasoning that tomorrow's prey
may be a mouse
(why is a mouse more acceptable?)
no philosophies
only the certain knowledge:

Next summer, you will be more careful.
Next summer, you will look down.

To Dorothy from Oz in Autumn

I didn't know that you would step
into the night before me
that darkness would swallow
your bright laughter
and taint the gladdest memory
with sorrow
that everything would fall
into that gulf
between

when people die
we make up destinations
lily-strewn and fragranced
with rosaries of prayers
whispered by us poor travelers
here below

when people disappear
they drift in limbo
marauding ghosts
that ambush sleep
and waylay the smallest moment's joy
placing memories like stones
beneath the mattress

sometimes it takes no more
than a stray bead
found behind the sofa
or a matted hairbrush
discovered in cleaning
to trigger weeks
of bootless searching
voices that echo

softly now and then
from out of nowhere
fading back to silence
accusations, arguments
past midnight
eternal questions
of where and why
and what we might have said

when you were four
and so afraid
of kindergarten monsters
I lifted your bangs
planted a ruby Oz kiss
on your forehead
a Glinda Good Witch spell
to keep you safe

a child your faith was strong
in me and Revlon
your teacher told
how all day long
you'd peek into the mirror
reassure yourself
then run back out to play

as seasons change
I find you all around me
in caramel and apple afternoons
in Monarchs who sojourn
a day or two
winged additions to trees
already burning
an overkill of beauty

before the turn to grey
and damp is on us
before the winter chill
takes hold for good
and brings to silence
even the last chance
all-forgiving breath

wherever you are now
in hell or heaven
some lonely bar
or back against the wall
find a mirror, child
see the reflection
upon your forehead
stained indelible
the promise
that remains.

Sun in Aries, Amelia rising

for my daughter

Sky-eyed wind dancer
daughter of wings and wonder
you sprang forth from me
like butterflies
from a dark cavern

perhaps it was my obsession
nine long months
with Amelia-the-unconfinable
fetterless, headstrong
perpetually waving good-bye

perhaps it was my hidden desire
to follow her fearless
flight to nowhere but away
that tangled my DNA
as I knit your bones

and so it was no surprise
when you drove me to an airfield
in early light
showed me
the winged passion
you'd fed in secret

tall and lanky girl
you folded yourself into the cockpit
that cradled you stronger
than a mother's arms
took off
looped, dived
brushed the ground

stirring dust that blinded me
and all that time
laughter drifted down
as though to mock me
still

I knew Amelia
had won out
that sky
had claimed you

now these many years gone
my static-voiced
reason long faded
somewhere you fly free
coordinates inconsequential
not caring much
what is sky
or sea
the horizon seductive
or the shelter
tame and tedious
that is Howland
or me.

Orchard

for Sarah
Not all those who wander are lost. – JRR Tolkien

From blossom
to sticky green
of early leaves
and sugary fruition
these orbs grow
fat and freckled, nectar-swelled
fully-fleshed and pendulous
sweet-pulped delight
of tree-climbing children
and vagrant wannabes
who cut a wide swath
around apples on the table
responding instead
to wild desire
to choose and pluck
one's own
to feel
that perfect weight
within the hand
unspoiled as yet
by insect or by worm --
to understand.

God save the errant child
compelled to relish both
the succulent forbidden
and the blest.

Seeker

Others more fortunate
blessed with less
inquiring minds
dream of peaches
heavy-honeyed
free of pits
hanging low and seductive
in some halcyon orchard
together they follow
the distant Elysian call
of harps, angelic voices, salvation
for sheep oblivious
yet hungry
for a centre that will hold

solitary I wander
famished and bent
on a fruitless odyssey
peeling the artichoke of myth
leaf by concealing leaf dipped
in opiate butter
that only serves to mask
the hidden choke .
something solid to offer
the graybeard when it's my turn
to board the passing ferry
that stops for nothing.

The frozen butterfly

There, against the garden wall
caught in a tangle of leaf and vine
brittle with unexpected frost
this late Monarch
stopped in honeyed ecstasy
of fall and flower
imprisoned there beneath an icy glaze.

In that final moment
did it stop to see
the blossom gigantic and entire
as I draw back now,
seeing whole
the great, gifted earth
from which I sate myself
with this season's elixir?

Is this the way I, too, shall fall
drunken and drowsy
senses overburdened
drifting on wings made heavy with
nectar and delight
to spiral down
through the burning delirium
of autumn and untimely frost
to witness in that crystalline moment
the light fracture
prism
illuminate
some new and perfect garden
and there fall stunned and silent
never to fly again,
to fly forever.

November

Trees unleaving
in this small, mild rain
make mockery of spring,
when blossoms fell
covering the path
with green and gold renewal
now limbs relinquish
what they held,
let fall
the remainder

Women conceal
what we can
tears
disappointments

Eternal Emily-words
irremediable
we place in a keepsake box
for masochistic evenings
when there's a certain song
or too much wine
or too little everything
when we untie
all the neat little ends
we thought we'd taken care of

For now
coat zipped tight
against the coming chill
we face
what we must
and walk toward winter.

Juried exhibit

What's that in the upper right corner? I'm sensing repressed mother issues.

Oh please — put away the Freud — it's so outmoded — and this is anything but repressed.

The rage! The passion! Brushstrokes belie an animus that has not been properly integrated.

Hang psychology. I'm inclined to compare it to Miro.

You compare everything to Miro.

Thoughts as to what the fanged banana symbolizes? Anyone?

Is that a slash in the canvas? Was that intentional?

Someone put a bandaid across it — was it the artist? Makes it three dimensional. Interesting.

So much blood. So much angst.

Is that a woman under the serpent? Is that a serpent?

Brilliant.

It must be — too enigmatic to be anything else.

Stunning.

Oh, yes — this one has quite a future!

Has my vote!

Done!

Owlish artist from his darkened corner:
                          Mouse bones. Teeth. A hank of hair.

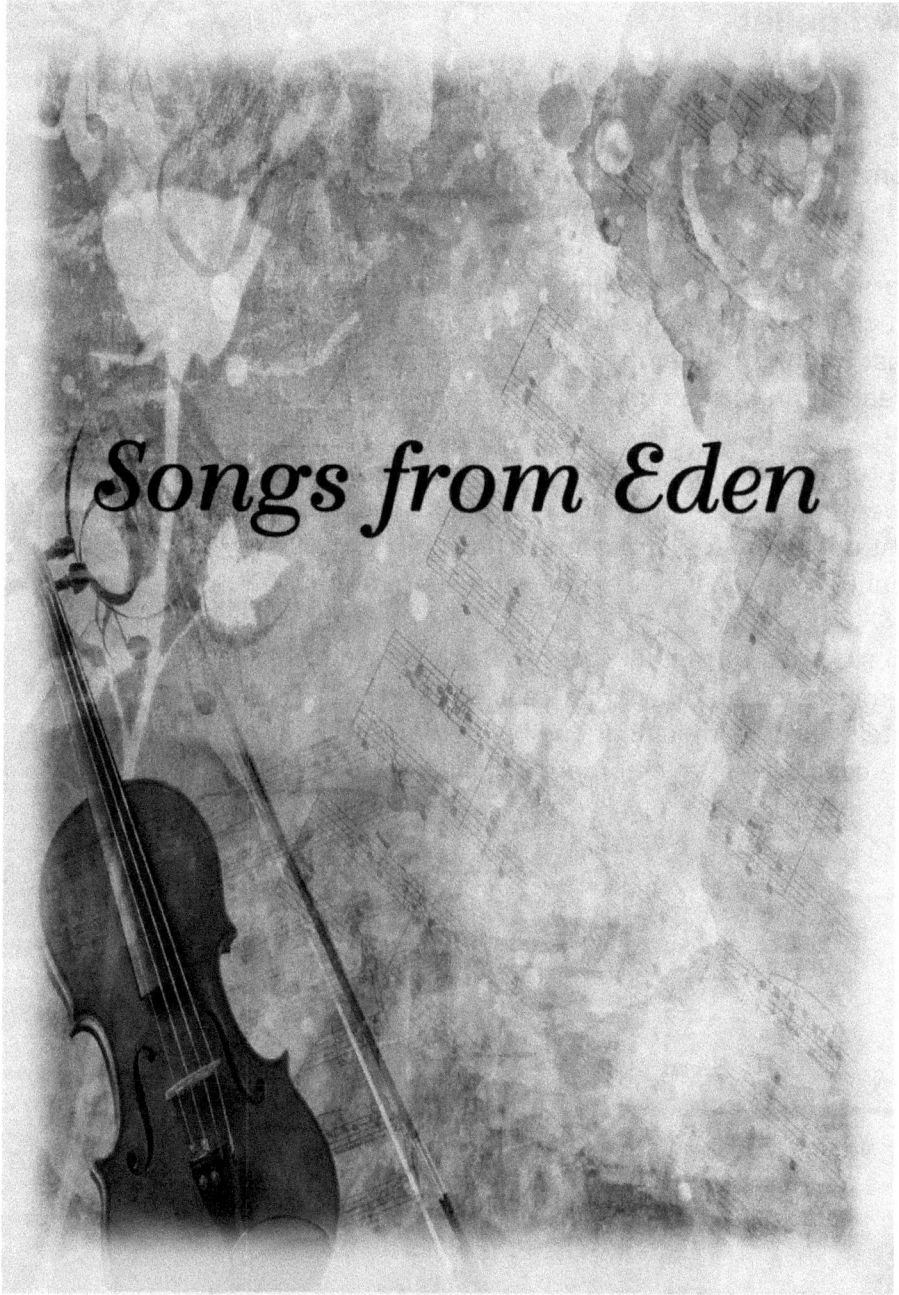

Songs from Eden

Owl pellet

Life serves a feast not readily digested,
designed to make us wiser, brave and strong;
some dishes are not easily divested
but linger in the system far too long.

Harsh words and brutal memories come to haunt us,
stuck in the gullet like a herring bone,
past midnight, they return to tease or taunt us,
creating an obstruction hard as stone,

all tangled with once-happy recollections —
sweet blue-eyed mornings, summer's mayfly love,
lost opportunities, gross imperfections —
it burdens wings that might have soared above;

till sickened in the darkness, blankly staring,
sequestered on our perch, cast all apart,
fate's feckless machinations boldly daring,
we cough it up, and someone calls it art.

Heart's Treasure

I cannot hold the colours of the sky.
Pale dawn escapes and brightens into noon,
and swift, vermilion wings of sunset fly
to silvery dominions of the moon.

Each bird may improvise within its song,
and rose or maple change at every glance —
the spectacle, the music that belong
to Nature lost in quick, chameleon dance.

And your love, holy in its gilded hour,
must in the dance of changes have its part,
must alter as the common leaf or flower:
such things become the treasure of the heart.

There, vigilant, I guard remembered gold,
the bounty mortal hand could never hold.

Gathered in

Now autumn with her meditative sigh
sweeps cool across the fields of harvest grain
the cider press awaits, the pumpkins lie
abundant, blest by fertile earth and rain

with summer's heated passion finally spent
the logs are stacked anticipating snow
while leaves abandon limbs in bright descent
all burnished with an incandescent glow

the world's at rest, the year is winding down
as nature burns the residue away
and smoky incense hallows farm and town
while cricket vespers rise at close of day

a book, a purring cat, a pot of tea
oh, tell me, April, what are you to me?

Trial

For the legions of women slaughtered and defamed in the name of God.

Those hard commandments placed in human hands,
appropriately carved upon a stone,
provoke the worst in those who are inclined
to punish what they cannot understand.
And so it was that I stood there at last
before the temple courts in Galilee.

I felt no shame before these Pharisees
who dragged me from my sweet beloved's bed
into the blinding light and choking dust,
nor that they shoved me naked, ridiculed
before a crowd that lusted for revenge
against a woman who had only done
what they did every night within their dreams.
And yet I felt such shame to be a pawn
to snare a man more innocent than I.

They put the question to him clear and plain:
In Moses' name, should they not stone me now?

I saw him bent and writing in the dust,
each mark undoing what the tablets said,
each mark unwinding every tangled word,
each mark replacing punishment with grace.
Then finally he spoke his fair reply
that he without a sin should cast the first.

I watched them drop their stones and walk away
all seething at this man's audacity
and yet still struck with wonder at his words.
I waited there to gather up the stones,
I took them home and made of them a cairn.

The Viewing

For my mother

You didn't look like anyone I knew
tucked in that casket like a Dresden doll
surrounded by a cloud of frigid blue
with cheeks more ruddy than a gangster's moll

The autumn in your hair had faded grey
I thought how you'd have hated to be seen
with makeup all awry and dressed that way
unlike the cover girl you'd always been

You didn't look like anyone I knew
Where were your fancy shoes, your Sunday best
And where the gloves that were a part of you
that faintest breath of scotch, and all the rest

You did not die; I did not misconstrue
You didn't look like anyone I knew.

Hallowed

Within each heart there is a sacred hall
by Hermes sealed against the world outside
where memories come to make a curtain call
where truth and cherished legend coincide

the Light of God's own robe bestows a grace
that glosses over any hurt we knew
no bitterness nor wound can have a place
with such illumination shining through

the laughter of a child, a lock of hair
beloved voices echo down the hall
each moment to relive is waiting there
where nothing loved is ever lost at all

there, we can go where paths might well have led
and speak the things we wish we could have said.

My grandmother's garden

for Carla Montine Howell Gunn

The drive past Haven Court and Ganymede
reveals a garden wild and out of place
with no regard to color, height, or weed
spontaneous, its dance, a gypsy's grace

I think of you each time I pass that street
and on occasion, go out of my way
to simply glimpse a garden not-so-neat
when topiary offerings rule the day

You grew your gardens rampant, unconfined
were loathe to prune them back or manicure
but loved each petal as it was designed
each leaf, the product of Divine couture

We children so attended will recall
you cherished wayward blossoms most of all.

About the Poet

Nine times nominated for The Pushcart Prize, Carla Martin-Wood is the author of the recently released *Into the Windfall Light* from The Pink Petticoat Press. She is also the author of *Flight Risk & Other Poems, How we are loved, Songs from the Web [encore],* and *One flew east*, all from Fortunate Childe Publications.

She has authored seven chapbooks: *Songs from the Web* (Bitter Wine Press); *Garden of Regret* and *Redheaded Stepchild* (both Pudding House Chapbook Series); *Feed Sack Majesty, HerStory,* and *The Last Magick and Other Poems* (all Fortunate Childe Publications); and *Absinthe & Valentines* (Flutter Press).

A copy of Carla's chapbook, *Garden of Regret,* resides in the Special Collections & University Archives at Stanford University, contributed by Yevgeny Yevtushenko. Carla's poems have appeared in a plethora of journals and numerous anthologies in the US, England, and Ireland since 1978.

Carla is Copy Director of an advertising agency. She has three magnificent granddaughters: Sarah, Erica, and Caeli Grace, in order of appearance. Carla was nominated for Best of the Net 2010 and 2011, and is listed in the Poets & Writers Directory at www.pw.org.

Acknowledgements

Heart's Treasure first appeared in *The Lyric*
False Spring and *For Mary Jane* first appeared in *Flutter Poetry Journal*
The Least of These first appeared in *Joyful*
Way of the Raven first appeared in *ken*again*
Medusa, Circe, Genesis, Immortal, and *Wicked* first appeared in *Tipping the Sacred Cow: a Fortunate Childe Anthology* (Fortunate Childe Publications 2011)
Lilith first appeared in *Lilith: a collection of women's writes,* a Fortunate Childe Anthology (Fortunate Childe Publications 2009)
Magdalen first appeared in *The Victorian Violet Poetry Journal*
Eve first appeared in *Garden of Regret* (Pudding House Chapbook Series)
Comet first appeared in *tinfoildresses*
Too Late, Don't tell the Children, Don't tell Mama, and *Prodigal* first appeared in *Poets for Living Waters*
Owl Pellet, Gathered in, Hallowed, and *My grandmother's garden* first appeared in *Into the Windfall Light* (The Pink Petticoat Press 2011)

In 2010, Fortunate Childe Publications re-released *Songs from the Web* for a limited time. This was a republication of the original 1986 chapbook, with additional poems included. This book has now been retired, and some of the poems have been included in this collection. They are: *Bedtime story, Song for Prometheus, Seeker, For Dean, Linguist, Purple hull peas, Fall, To Dorothy from Oz in Autumn, Sun in Aries, Amelia rising, Orchard, Lady at the Window, November*

Also by this author

How we are loved
Fortunate Childe Publications

Into the Windfall Light
The Pink Petticoat Press

Flight Risk & Other Poems
Fortunate Childe Publications

One flew east
Fortunate Childe Publications

Songs from the Web (encore)
Fortunate Childe Publications

Absinthe & Valentines
Flutter Press

The Last Magick
Fortunate Childe Publications

HerStory
Fortunate Childe Publications

Feed Sack Majesty
Fortunate Childe Publications

Redheaded Stepchild
Pudding House Chapbook Series

Garden of Regret
Pudding House Chapbook Series

www.ingramcontent.com/pod-product-compliance
Lightning Source LLC
Chambersburg PA
CBHW071130090426
42736CB00012B/2074